WORLD OF WOW WONDER

I KNOW ABOUT!

Children will be WOWed when they dive into this fun, fact-packed series that explores the most fascinating things in the world around them. From the human body, to sharks, to insects, to atlases, to dinosaurs, there is something new and exciting to learn at every turn!

These books are anchored by the philosophy that the best form of learning is through high-quality, multi-faceted experiences. This series provides lasting knowledge as it engages children on many levels. The graphics and illustrations inspire learning in readers of all ages as they explore everything from the depths of the ocean to the cells of the human body. Students will also be captivated by the fun facts and interesting explanations, which bolster a comprehensive understanding of each subject area.

Teachers and parents alike will appreciate the significance of this series as an addition to their libraries as it promotes self-sufficiency in the learning process. With vividly portrayed information on all of children's favorite subjects, these books promote an enjoyment for both discovering and sharing knowledge, key components of a successful learning environment.

Learning should be fun, interesting, and applicable, and we are sure the young learners in your life will find this series to be all of that – and more!

"You can teach a student a lesson for a day; but if you can teach him to learn by creating curiosity, he will continue the learning process as long as he lives."

– Clay P. Bedford

© 2014 Flowerpot Press

Contents under license from
Aladdin Books Ltd.

Flowerpot Press
142 2nd Avenue North
Franklin, TN 37064

Flowerpot Press, a Division of Kamalu LLC, Franklin, TN, U.S.A. and Flowerpot Children's Press, Inc., Oakville, ON, Canada.

ISBN 978-1-77093-930-1

Author:
Jane Walker

Designer:
David West

Series Director:
Bibby Whittaker

Editor:
Jen Green

Picture Research:
Emma Krikler

Illustrators:
Ian Thompson
Cartoons by Tony Kenyon.

American Edition Editor: Johannah Gilman Paiva
American Redesign: Jonas Fearon Bell

Printed in China.

CONTENTS

I KNOW ABOUT!
SHARKS

By Jane Walker

Illustrated By Ian Thompson

Cartoons By Tony Kenyon

FLOWERPOT PRESS
NASHVILLE · TORONTO

Sharks are meat-eating fish that are found all around the world. There are more than 350 different kinds of sharks. They range in size from the huge whale shark to tiny sharks that can fit in the palm of your hand. Although many sharks are fierce hunters, the biggest sharks, like the whale shark and the basking shark, are gentle creatures. Basking sharks eat only the tiny plants and animals that drift in the sea.

Tiny sharks

The tiny dwarf shark is only about 5.5 inches long when fully grown. Lantern sharks and dogfish are other kinds of small sharks.

LEOPARD SHARK

Huge sharks

Whale sharks are the biggest fish in the world. An adult whale shark can be up to 40 feet long. They may weigh more than 14 tons, which is about twice as heavy as an adult African elephant.

WHALE SHARK

Shark names
Several kinds of sharks are named after wild animals because of the markings on their skin. These include leopard sharks, zebra sharks, and tiger sharks. Hammerhead sharks got their name from their strangely shaped heads. Blue, great white, grey reef, and lemon sharks are simply named after the color of their skin.

MAKO SHARK

Fast swimmers
Mako sharks and porbeagles have smooth, sleek bodies and tails that are specially suited to moving quickly through the water. A mako shark can swim at great speed, sometimes leaping clear of the water.

Sharks are some of the most powerful and fearsome creatures in the sea. They come in lots of different shapes and sizes. Many have streamlined bodies that help them swim quickly and easily. Sharks do not have scales like bony fish. Instead, their bodies are rough and covered in tiny, thornlike points called "denticles," or skin-teeth.

Skeletons

Most fish have a skeleton made of bones. But a shark's skeleton is made of a tough, flexible material called "cartilage." Bony fish also have a special gas-filled bag, called a "swim bladder," to keep them afloat in the water. Sharks have no swim bladder, and have to keep swimming to avoid sinking.

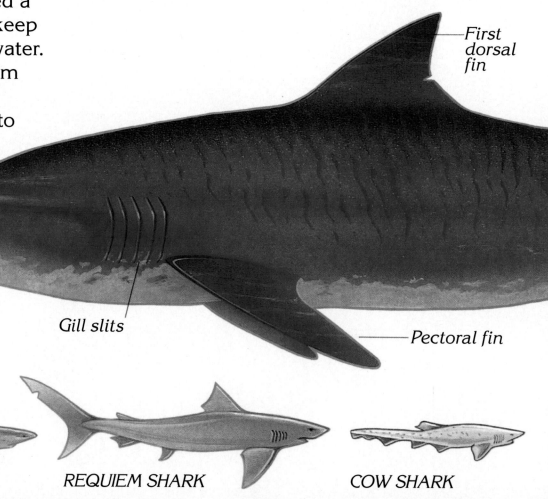

TIGER SHARK

Gill slits

First dorsal fin

Pectoral fin

BRAMBLE SHARK

REQUIEM SHARK

COW SHARK

Fins

Most sharks have two sets of paired fins, as well as two fins on their back and a smaller fin on the underside of the body. The large triangular-shaped fin (dorsal fin) on a shark's back can sometimes be seen above the water's surface. Fins help the shark to balance and steer as it swims through the water.

—Denticles

—Second dorsal fin

Streamlining

The streamlined shape of most sharks helps them to swim easily through the water. A streamlined shape is rounded and blunt at the front, and pointed at the back. Water flows smoothly past it. Use stiff cardboard to make a shape like the one below, as well as a rounded shape like a cylinder. Test to see which shape moves more easily through water.

—Caudal fin

Shark tails

Sharks bend their tails from side to side to push their bodies through the water.

Anal fin

Pelvic fin

ROUGH SHARK

THRESHER SHARK

BLIND SHARK

Sharks live in the world's oceans and seas, from the chilly Arctic Ocean to the warm tropical waters off Africa. Some sharks live in the deepest part of the ocean, while others spend most of their time near the surface. Nurse sharks stay near the coast, but most sharks live far out to sea.

The greatest traveler

Blue sharks travel long distances in the tropical waters and warm, temperate seas of the Atlantic Ocean. Blue sharks from the north Atlantic have been found more than 3,700 miles away, off the coast of South America.

Above and below

Basking sharks and thresher sharks swim along the water's surface looking for food. Carpet sharks and horn sharks live on the seabed. Swell sharks rest on the ocean floor during the day, and hunt for food at night. Hammerhead sharks often come to the surface in groups of 100 or more, before swimming off to another part of the ocean.

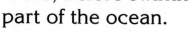

Island legends

People on many of the islands in the Pacific Ocean have worshipped sharks for thousands of years. In New Guinea, no one was allowed to kill a shark to avoid offending the gods of the sea. The people of Hawaii worshipped a shark king called "Kamo Hoa Lii." Some Pacific Islanders believed that sharks contained the spirits of their dead relatives.

SEA SPIRIT

Leaving the sea

Bull sharks sometimes leave the sea altogether and swim into freshwater rivers and lakes. They have been found in lakes and rivers in Central and South America, India, and the United States. Bull sharks have been spotted in the River Zambezi in Africa, at least 125 miles away from the sea.

IT'S A SHARK'S LIFE!

Sharks can see, hear, smell, taste, and touch—just like people. Hammerhead sharks have good eyesight and can see clearly in the deep, dark waters of the ocean. They can see all around when swimming along because their eyes are set on the tips of their hammer-shaped heads. Sharks also have a very good sense of hearing. They can only hear low-pitched noises, but these sounds travel long distances underwater.

Feeling for food

barbels

Nurse sharks, wobbegongs, and bamboo sharks (above) all have special feelers, called "barbels," on either side of their nose. They use them to feel their way along the seabed in search of food.

Special senses

A special sensing line runs along both sides of a shark's body, from its head all the way down to its tail. This is called a "lateral line." It helps the shark to detect prey, and anything moving in the water, such as other fish and sharks.

Nostril

Pores

Tiny skin holes, or pores, around a shark's head pick up electric signals from other fish, helping the shark to find its prey.

Sharks have a THIRD EYELID that protects their eyes when they bite.

LATERAL LINE

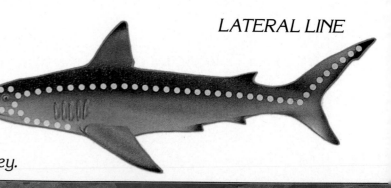

Staying alive

Like all animals, sharks need oxygen to stay alive. They get their oxygen from sea water. The water goes in through their mouth and flows over tiny featherlike parts behind the skull, called "gills." The gills remove the oxygen. When sharks swim, water flows over their gills and out through their gill slits. Most sharks have five pairs of gills. Angel sharks, which live on the seabed, get their oxygen by taking in water through special holes on the top of their head.

Shark friends

Fish called "remoras" attach themselves to sharks with a special sucker on the top of their head. They get a free ride from sharks, but in return they eat the tiny creatures living in the sharks' skin.

Small, stripy, pilot fish also swim close to sharks. People used to think that these fish guided the sharks toward their food. In fact, they probably swim along in shoals beside sharks for protection.

REMORA

LEOPARD SHARK

PILOT FISH

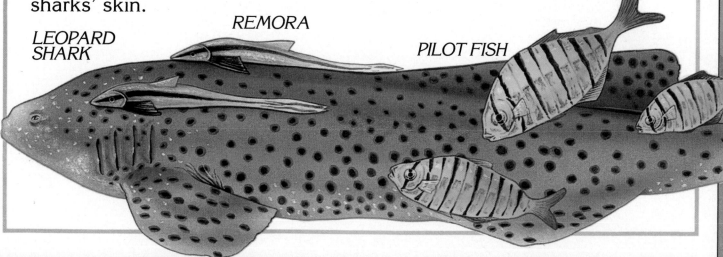

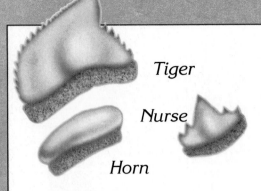

Tiger

Nurse

Horn

Teeth

Sharks have different kinds of teeth to suit the food they eat. Horn sharks have strong, flat teeth to crush the shells of crabs and other shellfish. Tiger sharks have sharp, jagged teeth to stab at and tear off pieces of food.

Most sharks have several rows of teeth. Broken teeth are quickly replaced by new sharp ones.

Most sharks use their sharp teeth to eat fish and other smaller kinds of shark. But the biggest sharks of all, the basking sharks and whale sharks, have a very different diet from most sharks. They feed on tiny animals and plants, called "plankton," that float in the sea.

Power jaws

When a shark bites, its jaw moves forward so that its teeth stick out. This makes it easier for the shark to snatch its prey. The shark then grips its victim in between its powerful jaws, to stop it escaping. Although the jaws of the megamouth shark measure more than one yard across, this gentle giant eats tiny shrimps and plankton.

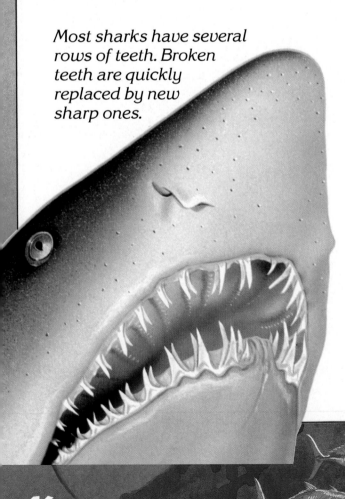

Staying alive

Like all animals, sharks need oxygen to stay alive. They get their oxygen from sea water. The water goes in through their mouth and flows over tiny featherlike parts behind the skull, called "gills." The gills remove the oxygen. When sharks swim, water flows over their gills and out through their gill slits. Most sharks have five pairs of gills. Angel sharks, which live on the seabed, get their oxygen by taking in water through special holes on the top of their head.

Shark friends

Fish called "remoras" attach themselves to sharks with a special sucker on the top of their head. They get a free ride from sharks, but in return they eat the tiny creatures living in the sharks' skin.

Small, stripy, pilot fish also swim close to sharks. People used to think that these fish guided the sharks toward their food. In fact, they probably swim along in shoals beside sharks for protection.

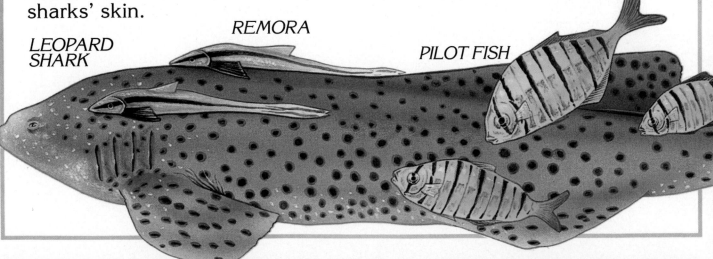

LEOPARD SHARK

REMORA

PILOT FISH

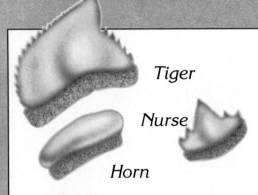

Tiger

Nurse

Horn

Teeth
Sharks have different kinds of teeth to suit the food they eat. Horn sharks have strong, flat teeth to crush the shells of crabs and other shellfish. Tiger sharks have sharp, jagged teeth to stab at and tear off pieces of food.

Most sharks have several rows of teeth. Broken teeth are quickly replaced by new sharp ones.

Most sharks use their sharp teeth to eat fish and other smaller kinds of shark. But the biggest sharks of all, the basking sharks and whale sharks, have a very different diet from most sharks. They feed on tiny animals and plants, called "plankton," that float in the sea.

Power jaws
When a shark bites, its jaw moves forward so that its teeth stick out. This makes it easier for the shark to snatch its prey. The shark then grips its victim in between its powerful jaws, to stop it escaping. Although the jaws of the megamouth shark measure more than one yard across, this gentle giant eats tiny shrimps and plankton.

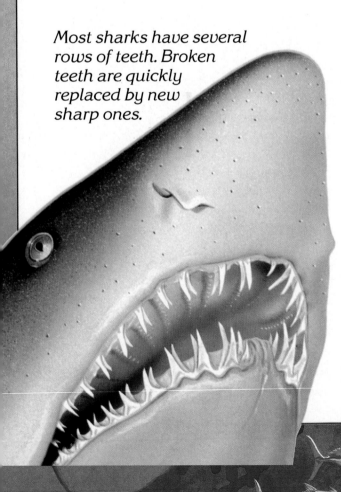

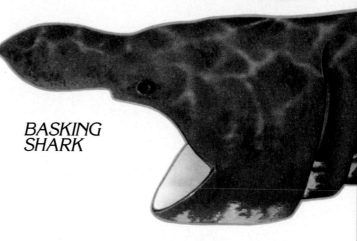

Filter feeding

Basking sharks and whale sharks take in huge mouthfuls of water and filter out the plankton. Because of the way they feed, these sharks are called "filter feeders."

BASKING SHARK

What's on the menu? Shark food ranges from tiny plankton to mammals, such as porpoises and sea-lions. As well as eating live fish, larger sharks eat sea creatures like dolphins, seals, and turtles, as well as seabirds.

SEA URCHIN

TURTLE

Strange things to eat

The tiger shark is sometimes called "the trash can of the sea." As well as eating poisonous sea snakes, hard-shelled sea turtles, or jellyfish, they also eat trash that has been thrown overboard from ships or has floated out to sea from the land.

Old tin cans, dogs, pieces of coal, and cardboard cartons have all been found inside tiger sharks.

JELLYFISH

In a FEEDING FRENZY sharks get overexcited by the smell of blood in the water and may attack each other.

Most sharks give birth to live babies called "pups." The eggs hatch inside the mother's body, and the newborn sharks come out alive. Other sharks, like dogfish, lay eggs. Once the mother shark has laid her eggs, she swims away, leaving the baby sharks to hatch on their own.

Finding a mate
Some sharks travel to special breeding grounds to find a mate. A male white-tip reef shark (above) chases after a female, playfully biting or grabbing hold of her fins with his teeth.

A baby SWELL SHARK is developing inside this leathery egg case.

Eggs
Shark eggs that are laid outside the female shark's body have tough, leathery cases. Cat-shark eggs are often attached to pieces of seaweed to stop the eggs from being washed away. Horn shark eggs are spiral-shaped. These sharks hide their eggs by pushing them into cracks in the rocks.

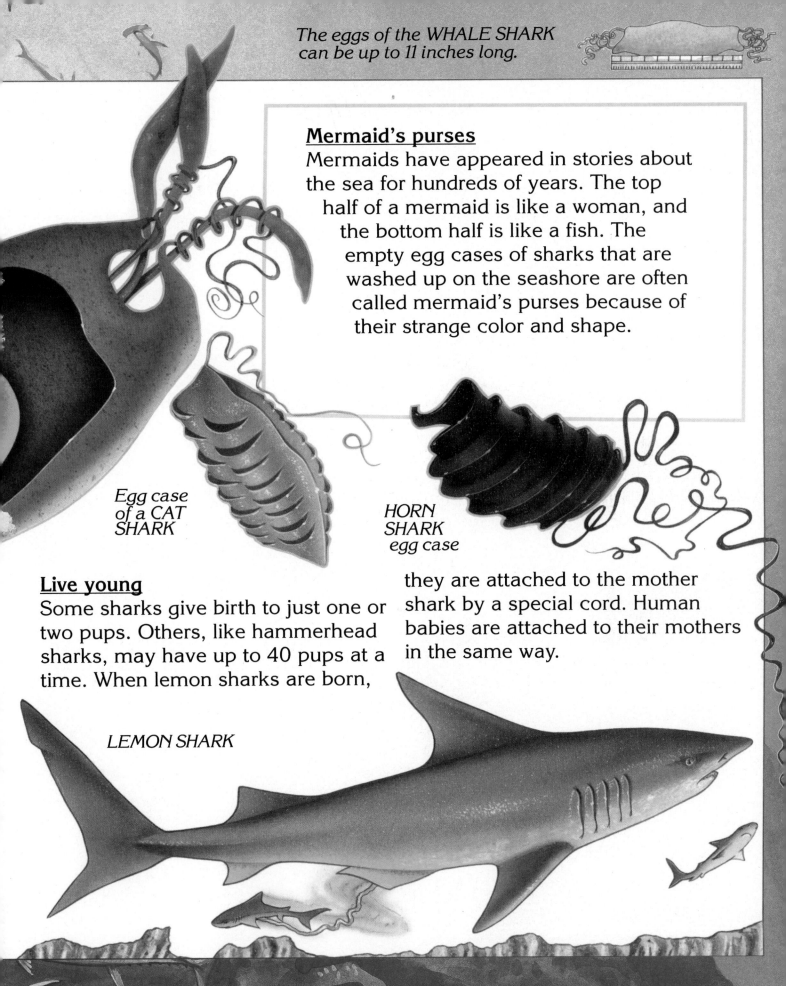

Mermaid's purses

Mermaids have appeared in stories about the sea for hundreds of years. The top half of a mermaid is like a woman, and the bottom half is like a fish. The empty egg cases of sharks that are washed up on the seashore are often called mermaid's purses because of their strange color and shape.

Egg case of a CAT SHARK

HORN SHARK egg case

Live young

Some sharks give birth to just one or two pups. Others, like hammerhead sharks, may have up to 40 pups at a time. When lemon sharks are born, they are attached to the mother shark by a special cord. Human babies are attached to their mothers in the same way.

LEMON SHARK

17

DANGEROUS SHARKS

Only about 50 of the 350 kinds of sharks are known to attack people in the water. Sharks mainly harm swimmers, surfers, and deep-sea divers. Some scientists think that sharks may mistake these people for seals or large fish. The most dangerous sharks are the great whites. These fierce and powerful hunters can be more than 20 feet long, and they have large, razor-sharp teeth.

Keeping safe

Some sharks swim close to the shore and attack people in the shallow water. In vacation resorts in Australia, South Africa, and along the west coast of the United States, bathers are protected from sharks by nets. These nets, which are made from steel mesh or from chains, help to prevent the sharks from swimming near to the shore.

Danger!

Other dangerous sharks include bull sharks, tiger sharks, and grey reef sharks. When angry, the grey reef shark arches its back and lowers the fins on the sides of its body. It behaves in this way when it is just about to attack its victim.

About 100 SHARK ATTACKS take place around the world each year. Many people survive these attacks, but they are sometimes left with terrible injuries.

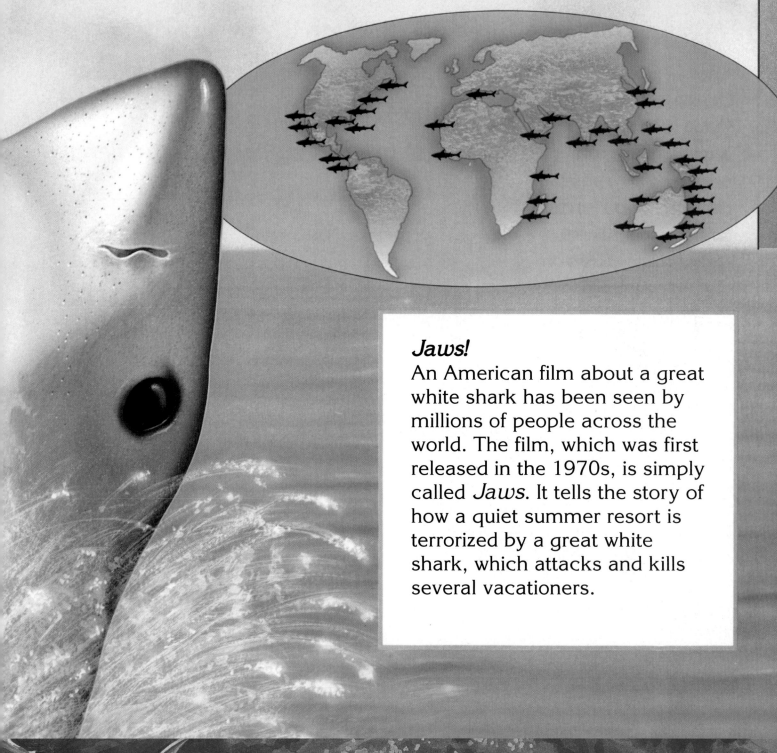

Jaws!

An American film about a great white shark has been seen by millions of people across the world. The film, which was first released in the 1970s, is simply called *Jaws*. It tells the story of how a quiet summer resort is terrorized by a great white shark, which attacks and kills several vacationers.

ANGEL SHARK

On the seabed

Nurse sharks live on the seabed, often moving only to catch a passing cuttlefish or to search for fish under nearby rocks. These sharks are also called "carpet sharks" and will not attack people unless provoked. Flat-bodied angel sharks also live at the bottom of the sea.

Most sharks are not dangerous at all. In fact, the biggest sharks of all, the whale sharks and basking sharks, are quite harmless. They will even allow divers to hold onto their fins and take a free ride through the water. These huge sharks are filter feeders (see page 15) and they do not have the sharp cutting teeth of the fierce attacking sharks, like the great white.

STARRY SMOOTH HOUND

CARPET SHARK

NURSE SHARK

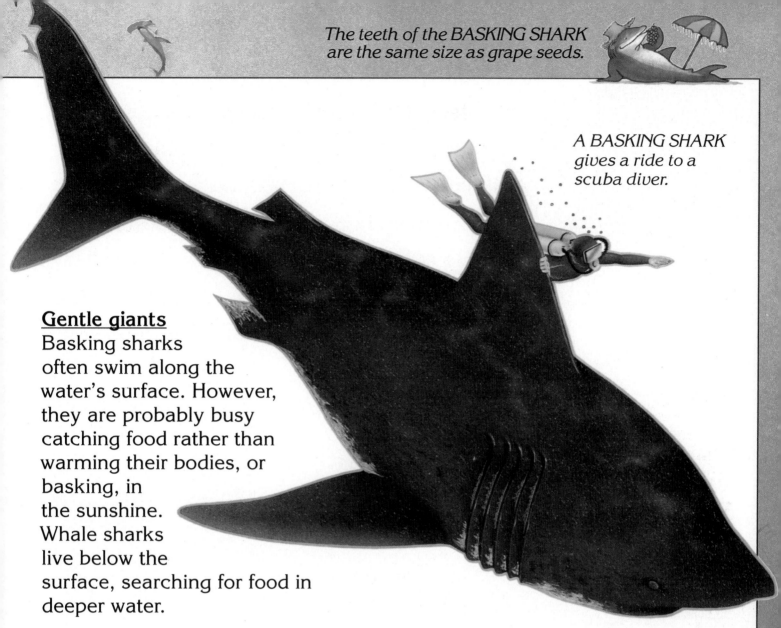

The teeth of the BASKING SHARK are the same size as grape seeds.

A BASKING SHARK gives a ride to a scuba diver.

Gentle giants

Basking sharks often swim along the water's surface. However, they are probably busy catching food rather than warming their bodies, or basking, in the sunshine. Whale sharks live below the surface, searching for food in deeper water.

What is camouflage?

Camouflage means being able to hide easily from others by blending in with your surroundings. On the seabed, the speckled skin of the angel shark helps it to hide in the sand. Swell sharks gulp down mouthfuls of water or air and then squeeze their bodies between the rocks.

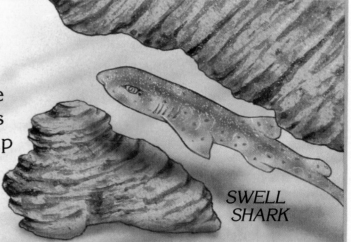

SWELL SHARK

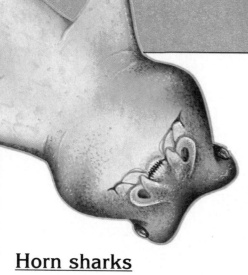

STRANGE SHARKS

One of the strangest-looking groups of sharks are the hammerheads. These odd fish have their eyes and nostrils at the ends of their wide, hammerlike heads. Another unusual shark is the frill shark, which has a collar of skin folds behind its head. This shark is also known as the "lizard-head."

Horn sharks
The Port Jackson shark (above) is one kind of horn shark. It lives in the warm waters of the Indian and Pacific Oceans. Port Jackson sharks are also known as "pig sharks" because of their square-shaped head and large nostrils.

HAMMERHEAD SHARK

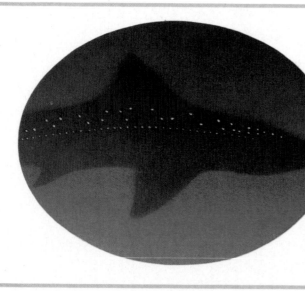

Shining in the dark
The tiny lantern shark lives deep down in the darkest parts of the ocean. Its small body glows in the dark water, even as far down as 6,500 feet below the surface. Lantern sharks have special parts on their bellies that give off light. Other sharks that glow in the dark are cookie cutters and green dogfish.

Rare sharks

Scientists know very little about some sharks, because they have only ever seen a small number of them. One of the rarest sharks is the goblin or elfin shark, which has a long pointed horn on the top of its head. A completely new kind of shark, the megamouth, was found off the coast of Hawaii in 1976. Fewer than 10 of these enormous sharks have ever been seen.

This rare GOBLIN SHARK lives in very deep water.

In disguise

Most carpet or nurse sharks live on the ocean floor in tropical seas. One of these is the wobbegong, which lives off the coasts of Australia as well as several Asian countries, including China, Vietnam, and Japan. Wobbegong is the shark's Aborigine name. These sharks are very well camouflaged. The blotchy markings and the color of their skin blend in with the rocks and corals around them. Even the bearded fringe below the wobbegong's mouth looks like strands of seaweed.

The ornate WOBBEGONG can easily hide among the corals and seaweed on the seabed.

The first sharks lived about 400 million years ago. But most of today's sharks are more like the ones that roamed the seas after the dinosaurs disappeared, about 65 million years ago. The giant megalodon shark, which was about 43 feet long, ruled the seas about 20 million years ago. Megalodons may still have been alive 12,000 years ago. Its closest relative alive today is the great white shark.

SHARK FOSSIL

Ancient sharks

The remains of the earliest known sharks have been found in the United States. When the sharks died, their bodies sank down onto the seabed and were preserved in layers of sand, mud, and rock. The buried remains of once-living things are known as fossils.

One of the most common of the early sharks, called CLADOSELACHE, lived around 350 million years ago.

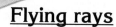

Flying rays

Rays use the huge wing-like fins on the sides of their body to swim through the water. They look as if they are really "flying" through the sea. They are filter feeders like basking sharks, eating the tiny plankton in the sea.

Shark cousins

Rays, skates, and sawfish belong to the same group of fish as sharks. Rays spend most of their time on the seabed, while sawfish are often found in freshwater rivers and lakes. The body of the ray is so broad that the width of its body is more than the length. Giant manta rays are sometimes more than 20 feet wide.

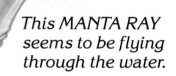

This MANTA RAY seems to be flying through the water.

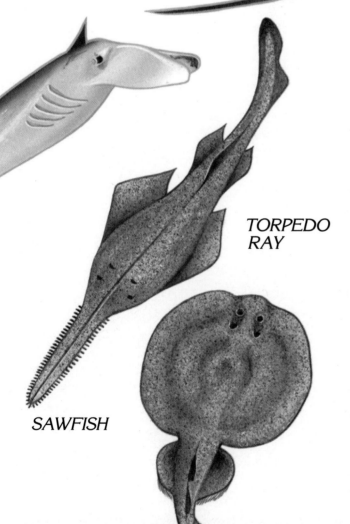

TORPEDO RAY

SAWFISH

The sting of the stingray

Stingrays were given their name because of the poisonous spines in their tails. These spines have tiny barbs along the edges. Stingrays use these spines to defend themselves against enemies, such as hammerhead sharks.

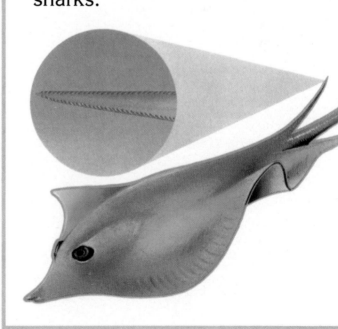

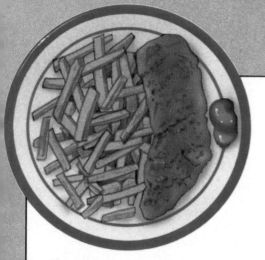

Food
The Chinese make a special soup from dried shark fins. Shark meat is eaten by people in many places around the world. In England, fried spiny dogfish (above) is sold in fish and chip shops.

All over the world, people have found different ways to make use of sharks. We capture sharks and take their flesh, skin, teeth, fins, and even their liver. Sharks provide people with food to eat, with skin to make into leather goods, with teeth to make into jewelry and decorations, and with oil that is used to manufacture skin creams, lipsticks, and pills. Shark fishing is a popular sport in the Caribbean and off the coasts of Australia and North America.

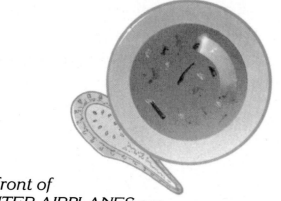

SHARK FIN soup

The front of FIGHTER AIRPLANES are sometimes painted with pictures of sharks' jaws to make them look frightening.

Sharks and medicine
In the past, the Romans treated teething pains by rubbing their children's teeth with dried shark brains. Scientists have found that sharks very rarely develop cancer. Today, cancer kills more than 5 million people in the world each year. Research into sharks may help doctors find a cure for this killer disease.

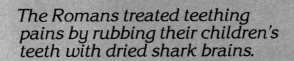

Sharks' enemies

Human beings are sharks' main enemies. Sharks are killed for sport or for their meat and oil. There is a danger that people are killing too many sharks, and some kinds may even disappear altogether. Dolphins and porpoises also attack sharks, and occasionally win the fight.

Shark products

Shark skin is made into a whole range of products, from boots and belts to sword handles and leather boxes. It is dyed and then polished to make it smooth. Rough shark skin is called "shagreen." It used to be used to smooth down wood and precious stones. Many Japanese people take shark oil pills to prevent heart disease and cancer. The oil, which comes from sharks' liver, is rich in vitamin A. But the same vitamin can now be made artificially, without having to kill sharks.

Many COSMETICS, such as anti-wrinkle skin creams and lipsticks, contain oil from sharks.

MORE FASCINATING FACTS

COOKIE CUTTER SHARKS take round bites out of their victims.

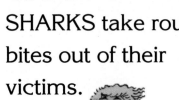

In the past, sailors attached a SHARK'S TAIL to the bow of their ship to bring them good luck.

During World War II, the Japanese used SHARK LIVER OIL in the engines of their fighter planes.

A BASKING SHARK can filter 2,376 gallons of water in 1 hour.

The GREY REEF SHARK swims in a figure eight when it is frightened.

Some AFRICAN TRIBESMEN protected their swords with covers made from shark skin.

On the Pacific island of Samoa, models of sharks were hung from PALM TREES to protect the fruit.

On some Pacific islands, shark teeth are used to make SKIN TATTOOS.

GLOSSARY

BARBEL A fingerlike feeler on the side of a shark's nose or jaw.

BASKING When referring to sharks, this means swimming near the surface of the water.

CAMOUFLAGE Being colored or shaped to blend in easily with your surroundings.

CARTILAGE A tough, flexible material that makes up the skeleton of sharks, skates, and rays.

DENTICLES The thornlike points covering a shark's body.

DORSAL On the back, as in a dorsal fin.

FILTER FEEDER Any sea creature that feeds by removing tiny plants and animals from sea water.

FIN Part of a fish that helps it to move, steer, or balance in water.

FOSSIL The remains of living things that lived millions of years ago.

GILLS Tiny featherlike parts inside the throat or behind the skull of a fish or shark that take oxygen out of water.

LATERAL LINE A special line along a shark's sides that helps it to detect movements in the water.

PECTORAL On the chest, as in a pectoral fin.

PLANKTON Small, often almost invisible, plants and animals that drift in the seas.

PORE A tiny hole in the skin.

PUP A newborn shark.

SPINE A hard, pointed part on a fish. It is often sharp and may contain poison.

STREAMLINED Having a smooth shape that will move easily through air or water.

SWIM BLADDER A special balloon-like bag filled with gas inside the body of bony fish. It helps fish to float in the water.

INDEX